Play
TABLE TENNIS

Whether righty or lefty, you can learn to play top table tennis following the clear and concise directions for service, return, attack, defense and strategy strokes demonstrated by left-handed table tennis star Glenn Cowan in easy-to-follow sequenced photographs.

Official United States Table Tennis Association rules, covering equipment, play and scoring for both singles and doubles playing, are included both as guidelines for playroom games and to ready you for official tournament matches.

Lastly, because playing and enjoying table tennis depends largely on conditioning the body to the rigors of play, fifteen exercises have been specially selected to help you to play your best from serve to point.

The book of
TABLE TENNIS
–how to play the game

Demonstrated by
GLENN COWAN

Over 100 Action Photographs

GROSSET & DUNLAP
A National General Company
Publishers New York

Library of Congress Catalog Card Number:70-186664
ISBN: 0-448-01517-X

Printed in the United States of America

Photos by Gene Trindl of Globe Photos

Table Tennis rules supplied through
the courtesy of Cyril Lederman, Chairman
of the Rules Committee for the United
States Table Tennis Association.

Contents

Introduction 8
Equipment 12
  Table 13
  Ball 13
  Racket 13
Grip 14
  Penhold 15
  Shakehands 16

How To Play

Service 19
  Cut (forehand/backhand) 20
  Topspin (forehand/backhand) 22
Return 24
  Of Long Service (forehand/backhand) 24
  Of Short Service (forehand/backhand) 29
Attack 31
  Smash (forehand/backhand) 32
  Loop Drive (forehand) 34
  Loop (backhand) 36
  Counter-Drive (backhand) 37
Defense 38
  Lob (forehand/backhand) 38
  Chop (forehand/backhand) 41
  Block (forehand) 43
Strategy 44
  Drop Shot (forehand) 45
  Drop Shot of Lob (forehand) 46
  Push (backhand) 47

Official (USTTA) Rules

Singles   50
  Equipment   51
  Play   52
  Scoring   54
  Ends and Service   55
Doubles   58
  Equipment   59
  Play   59
United States Table Tennis Association   61

Exercises

Warm-Up   64
  Head and Neck Rotation   65
  Horizontal Arm Rotation   66
  Finger Pull   67
  Palm Press   67
  Wrist and Finger Flex   68
  Knee Thrust   69
  Side Step   70
  Side Jump   71
  Ankle Twist   72
  Wrist Shake   72
Conditioning   73
  Around the House   73
  Toe Touch to Side   74
  Half Sit-Up with Partner   75
  Back Stretch with Partner   76
  High Jump   77

About Glenn Cowan   79

Introduction

Ably demonstrated by table tennis champion Glenn Cowan, here are the grips, the strokes and warm-up and conditioning exercises designed to help you to learn, play and enjoy that newly spotlighted, international sport of table tennis.

Because Glenn Cowan is left-handed, the sequenced photographs in the front, how-to-play section of this book have been printed twice—as photographed and "flopped"—so that both right-handed and left-handed players can see and easily follow the necessary movements. Though the accompanying text has been written toward left-handed players, right-handers need only refer to the *right* or *left* designations in parentheses to tailor the wording to their needs.

Lastly, this book doesn't pretend to fashion top table tennis players overnight. It is, however, a shove in the right direction. But winning player or no, the important thing to remember is that the real winners at table tennis are the ones who fight hard twenty-one points a game.

The book of
TABLE TENNIS
–how to play the game

Equipment

To play table tennis, all that is needed is a table with a net, a ball, and a pair of rackets. Some stores carry "toy" table tennis sets, including a net which can be attached to a kitchen table, for under $1.00. To play a serious game of table tennis, however, you should use the right equipment.

Regulation table tennis rackets and balls are still quite inexpensive. A good pimpled hard-rubber or sponge-rubber "sandwich" racket may run anywhere from $2 to $8.50, and "approved" or "official" balls can be purchased from most sports supply stores for between 15¢ and 35¢ each.

Clothing restrictions are minimal. White or unusually bright clothing should not be worn while playing as it is very hard to see the small white ball against that type of background. Wear comfortable clothing that does not bind, and shoes that will grip (rubber-soled is best) for safe play.

Table

A regulation table is nine feet long by five feet wide, rising to two and a half feet off the floor. The table top should allow an approved ball, dropped at a height of twelve inches, to bounce to a height of nine and a half inches. A six-inch-high, six-feet-long net is stretched tautly across the center of the table, between opponents. It is suspended between posts extending to six inches on either side of the table.

The table top should be stained (not painted, which slows down a ball) a dull, dark color, usually green. White lines around the edges of the table top allow players, in the heat of the contest, to readily ascertain playing space. A line down the center of the table separates the table into quarters for doubles playing.

Ball

Early table tennis balls were made of cork or rubber, but the ball normally in use today is a white, hollow, celluloid ball measuring between four and a half to four and three-quarter inches in circumference. Balls that meet play requirements are usually marked "official" or "approved."

The patented name of "Ping Pong," given to table tennis, is derived from the sounds made by the ball—"ping" as it was struck by a paddle, and "pong" when it hit the table.

Racket

Though rackets may vary in other ways—size, weight, color and shape (I have played in China with a *square* racket)—the most important difference between rackets is the type of rubber used to cover the wooden head. In competitive table tennis, the conventional "sandpaper" racket is illegal. A regulation racket must be covered with some type of rubber.

The simplest type of rubber used, very popular in the forties and fifties, is the hard "pimples-out" rubber. Though many top players, often with classic defensive strokes, still use hard-rubber rackets, most prefer the newer "sandwich" rackets with sponge rubber bonded to the wooden faces and a thin layer of either pimpled rubber or inverted pimpled rubber over it. A pimples-out sandwich racket is a good attacking racket. It allows good control, although the amount of spin is limited. The newest and most advanced racket, the inverted-pimples sandwich, is absolutely flat to the touch. The ball springs off this racket very quickly, and it takes a learned hand at table tennis to control it. The inverted sandwich, however, is the best type of racket for the loop drive, the most advanced shot in table tennis.

Lately, in both practice and tournaments, I have been using a mixed sandwich racket. It has pimples-out rubber on the backhand side for good control, and inverted pimpled rubber on the forehand side for a quick stroke with more spin.

Among top table tennis players, it is commonly believed that as the quality of the rubber used on rackets increases, so will the quality of competitive table tennis.

Grip

There are two basic kinds of grips, the penhold and the shakehands. Most Oriental players prefer the penhold, while European and American players are basically shakehands users. The penhold grip makes for a very strong forehand attacking shot, but the backhand is often quite weak. For this reason, top Oriental players train and condition their legs so that they can get into position quickly enough to take all shots with the forehand. Since the shakehands grip is better for a two-winged attack (or defense), shakehands users tend to play close to the center of the table and try to control the play in this manner.

Penhold Grip

This basically Oriental grip is formed by placing the thumb and index finger around the handle, much as if one were holding a pen. On the back, or non-playing side, the Japanese extend the fingers out along the side of the paddle or racket, which makes for a strong attacking forehand and a weaker backhand. In comparison, Chinese players grip the back with their fingers curled and closer together. This is better for close-to-the-table, two-sided attacking, which they vary with a strong backhand block.

RIGHT HAND   **LEFT HAND**

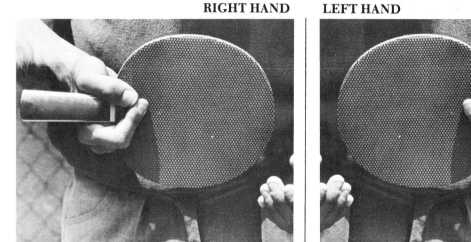

JAPANESE

CHINESE

Shakehands Grip

This grip, used by the top European and American players, is done by grabbing the racket handle naturally, as if shaking hands with it. The index finger is extended along the side of the racket to aid in control and power. On the forehand side, the thumb is placed wherever it is most comfortable.

Three variations of the forehand side of the grip are demonstrated here.

RIGHT HAND   **LEFT HAND**

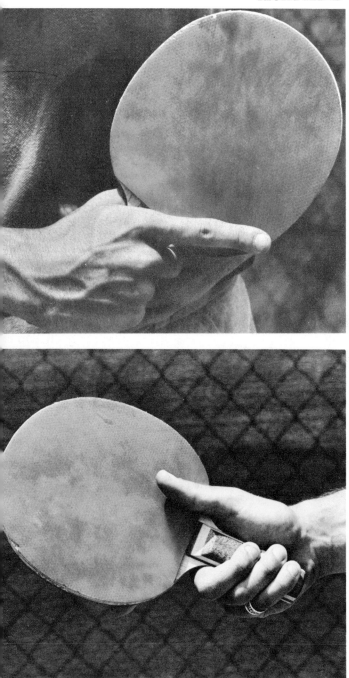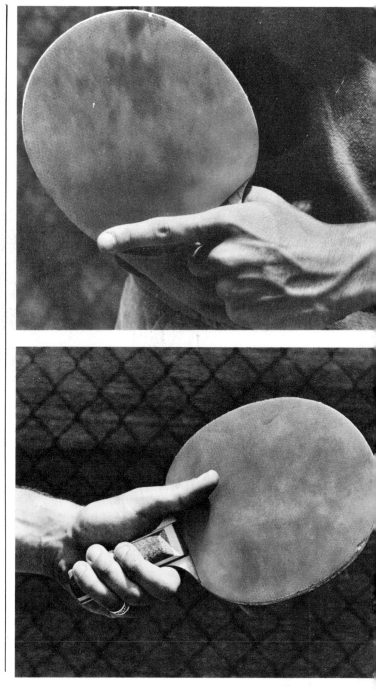

RIGHT HAND   **LEFT HAND**

HOW TO PLAY

Service

There are a number of ways to serve the ball. It is important strategy-wise, however, to begin each serve from the same stance so that the opponent will not be able to anticipate the kind of serve.

The basic service stance is with the knees slightly bent, the upper body crouched low, and weight primarily on the balls of the feet. The palm should be open and the ball in plain sight. Study the position and stance of your opponent and place the serve accordingly.

During a game, remember which serves work best against your opponent and use them again in the late, close stages of the game.

Forehand Cut

This is the basic forehand service. It may be served short or long, with a chop or with a sidespin.

Begin in the basic service position. For a stronger spin, the racket may be held further behind the ball. The ball is met with the racket moving counterclockwise under the ball. As the ball is hit, a sharp break of the wrist produces a chop, while a smooth motion of the arm produces a sidespin.

RIGHT HAND   **LEFT HAND**

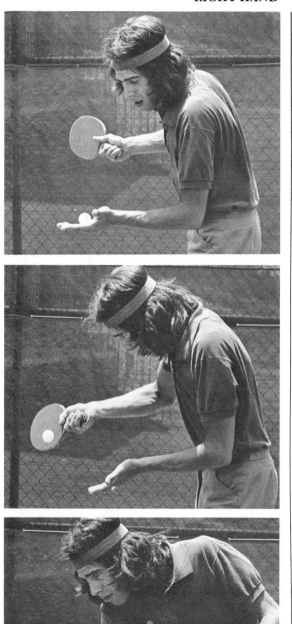

Backhand Cut

This is the basic backhand service. It may be served to either corner, to be followed by a loop or a smash.

Take the standard serving stance, and put the ball in the air. Break the wrist as the ball is hit so that the face of the racket cuts under the ball. The spin on the ball is controlled by the break of the wrist on contact. A sharp break puts a heavier chop on the ball. No break at all produces a sidespin or topspin.

RIGHT HAND   **LEFT HAND**

Forehand Topspin

This is a quick service used to begin an attack or to catch an opponent out of position. The user, however, should be ready to hit a deeper ball on the return.

Begin the same as with the cut service. As the ball is thrown upward, change the face of the racket from open (facing up) to closed (facing down). This is so the face will come over the ball, creating a fast topspin. With a correct follow-through, the racket finishes over the ball, as shown.

RIGHT HAND   **LEFT HAND**

Backhand Topspin

This is an even quicker serve than the forehand topspin, and used for the same purpose.

Begin in the standard service stance in order to guard against your opponent's anticipation of the spin. As the ball is thrown upward, bring the racket up behind the ball. Break the wrist forward as the ball is hit and allow the face of the racket to come up over the ball in the follow-through.

RIGHT HAND   **LEFT HAND**

Return

One of the keys to playing top table tennis is a good return of the serve. Keeping your eyes on the ball, assume the basic service-return stance. Stand loosely, with your weight forward and centered, legs flexed, and the body crouched and ready to move. Keep the upper body low for better following of the ball. Keep the arms extended for balance and the racket in front, ready to receive. Use the same starting position to receive all serves, so your opponent will not anticipate the return shot.

Forehand Return of Long Service

Get in service-return position. As the ball is served, step quickly to gain good position for the return. Remember to follow through, with the racket and body moving forward, eyes still following the ball.

RIGHT HAND   **LEFT HAND**

RIGHT HAND **LEFT HAND**

I usually stand by the corner of the table and attempt to hit all long serves with my forehand. I have let the ball drop here because my return is a spin shot.

RIGHT HAND   **LEFT HAND**

RIGHT HAND   **LEFT HAND**

Backhand Return of Long Service

Assume the basic service-return stance. If the ball is served to the backhand, it is important to take your time. Do not rush this shot. Get into a good position behind the ball before striking it.

RIGHT HAND   **LEFT HAND**

Forehand Return of Short Service

Possibly the most effective service is the short service to the forehand. Returning it not only involves good position and timing, but a delicate touch in order to return it short. Then the player must move quickly to get back into position to receive the next shot.

As the ball is served short, leave the basic service-return position and slide the left (right) leg towards the ball and under the table, keeping the body and eyes low. With the racket partially open, the ball is returned with a short, delicate, touch shot. Aim the ball as short as possible, with a brief follow-through coming close to the net. As the shot is completed, return immediately to ready position—the next shot will probably be a strong one.

RIGHT HAND   **LEFT HAND**

Backhand Return of Short Service

This return is handled much in the same manner as the forehand return of short service. As the ball is served short, leave the service-return position and slide the left (right) leg under the table. Keep the body low and the eyes right on the ball. Return the ball as short as possible, with a touch shot. After a short follow-through, remember to step back quickly, as the follow-up to the short service is often a long shot.

RIGHT HAND   **LEFT HAND**

RIGHT HAND **LEFT HAND**

Attack

There are many good attacking strokes, and here are five of the best.

I consider the smash the bread-and-butter shot of table tennis. It is the smasher, the finisher, the coup d'etat, if you will; the shot which delights the champs as much as the beginners.

The loop drive, similar to the defensive lob, has a smaller arc and a heavier topspin. The arc, although small, makes it a relatively safer attack shot than the offensive smash. In the last ten years, since the Orientals first introduced the loop drive, it has become the most common attacking stroke in Europe and Japan.

The counter-drive is the basic backhand attacking stroke. It is a quick, driving shot with less arc than any of the spin shots. It may be used just to keep the rally going while a player sets up for a smash, or kill, or to force a player out of position.

Forehand Smash

Begin in a crouched stance, with the left (right) leg slightly behind the right (left), legs spread comfortably apart. The racket starts open (face up), directly behind the ball at the height of the bounce. Meet the ball straight on, a little in front of the body. Break the forearm as the ball is covered, using the muscles of the side and shoulder to add to the power and effectiveness of the shot. As contact is made, shift your weight from the left to right (right to left) leg, bringing your whole body into the ball. The follow-through comes naturally, and should be the same after every stroke.

RIGHT HAND   **LEFT HAND**

Backhand Smash

As the ball comes to the backhand, move your right (left) leg slightly behind the other and concentrate the power in the right (left) thigh and side muscles. Bring the racket back behind the right (left) hip with the arm fully extended, turning the wrist back slightly for additional power. Try to contact the ball at the height of the bounce, with the forearm and the racket coming forward with full force. Follow through naturally, with the arm breaking after contacting the ball.

RIGHT HAND　　**LEFT HAND**

Forehand Loop Drive

Start with the knees bent, arms extended and racket at the ready. As the ball approaches, bring the open racket below the ball and up to hit it a little below the top of the bounce. As contact is made, shift your weight from your left (right) leg to your right (left) and break the arm, keeping your body low. Adjust your position and backswing according to the height and direction of the ball, always keeping the follow-through the same.

RIGHT HAND　　　**LEFT HAND**

Backhand Loop

With the knees bent, stand directly behind the ball. The ball should be hit from between three to five feet in back of the table, after the ball has reached the height of the bounce. The weight may be shifted on contact, if comfortable, but the topspin is gained with the moving of the arm and the flick of the wrist on contact. The amount of spin is determined by how much of the ball is hit, a good topspin being gained by merely brushing the ball.

RIGHT HAND **LEFT HAND**

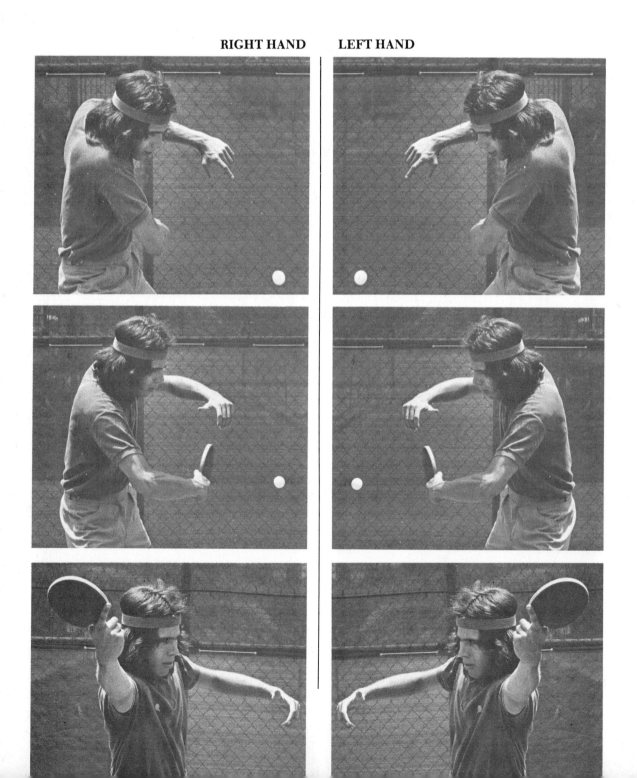

Backhand Counter-Drive

This stroke may be hit from right over the table, or from as far back as three feet. The weight may be shifted on contact, if desired, but this is not really necessary. The control comes mostly from the arm and wrist.

With the racket extended a little in front, and the body slightly crouched, take a short backswing directly behind the ball. Keep your eyes on the ball, and begin the forward stroke with the wrist and arm straight. Contact is made in front of the body. The racket comes quickly over the ball as the arm and wrist break, almost to a 90° angle. The follow-through brings your weight and the racket forward, with the arm extended. On finishing the stroke, return immediately to the ready, crouched, position.

RIGHT HAND   **LEFT HAND**

Defense

The lob is primarily a defensive shot, used when a player is forced far back from the table. Even strong attacking players may, at times, resort to this shot when forced out of their natural position. A good lobber, however, is able to use this shot to his advantage. While the ball may be very high and easily smashed, if the opponent must hit four or five hard lobs to win the point he is often too exhausted to play the next few points well. An expert lobber, furthermore, can actually make this high shot very difficult to hit. Hasse Alser of Sweden, for example, does this by placing it quite deep into the table, with varying degrees of topspin.

Another primary defensive stroke is the chop, and it is the more deceptive of the two. It is easier to break the wrist hard at the last minute with this shot and deliver a stronger chop than your opponent expects. In general, however, it is the less certain of the two strokes, because the footwork and positioning are more difficult.

Many defensive players aim to wear their receivers down by returning all of their opponents' best smashes. Today, however, top defensive players, such as Eberhard Scholar of Germany and Liang Ko-liang of China, win by changing or varying the spin of their defensive shots and forcing their attacking opponents into errors.

Forehand Lob

A high arc and good topspin are the key factors in this defensive stroke, with the spin being the more important of the two.

The forehand lob is usually made from at least five to seven feet away from the table, and quite often much further back. While awaiting the ball, the body is crouched, the left (right) leg in back of the right (left). During the backswing, the racket is lower than the ball, the racket coming up to contact the ball below the top of the bounce. The ball should not be hit solidly, but brushed to achieve a better spin. Shift the weight from the left to the right (right to the left) leg as the racket contacts the ball.

RIGHT HAND **LEFT HAND**

Backhand Lob

Crouch low and lean forward behind the ball as it approaches. Hold the racket low, timing your backswing to meet the ball about halfway up the body. The topspin is gained by the racket coming up fast as it meets the ball. As you follow through, adjust the speed and the height of the stroke in order to place the ball in the opponent's court.

RIGHT HAND   **LEFT HAND**

Forehand Chop

Start with a crouched stance, right (left) leg slightly in front, racket arm extended and the body leaning towards the ball. Hit the ball with the head of the racket as open as possible, stroking the racket under the ball to create the spin. The follow-through is not as long as with the backhand chop because it can naturally be stopped quicker. A shorter follow-through also aids in concealing from your opponent the spin given the ball on the shot.

RIGHT HAND   **LEFT HAND**

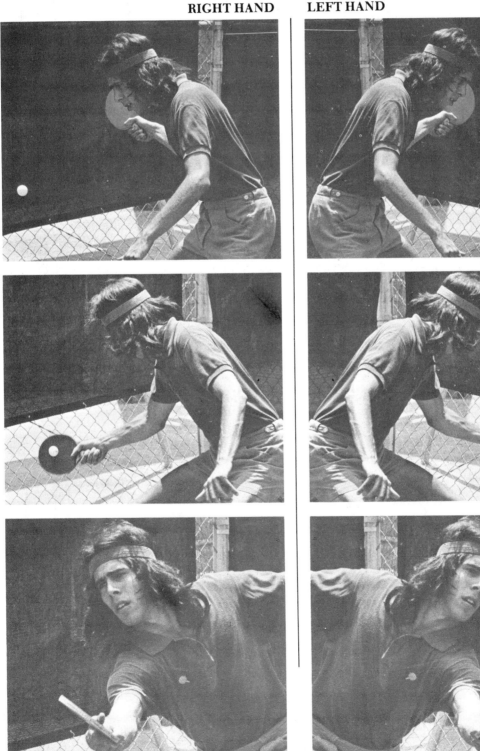

Backhand Chop

This is a defensive shot often used by receivers who normally play the entire game five to seven feet back from the table. Against harder attackers, however, a player might even be forced further back.

Start from a crouched stance, left (right) leg in front (though there are a few, famed *wrong foot* choppers), ready to lean in. As the racket slices under the ball, break the wrist. Here is where the spin is varied, from heavy chop to no spin at all, depending upon the break of the wrist. In the follow-through, the arm is extended almost fully, as the body turns to follow the direction of the ball.

RIGHT HAND   **LEFT HAND**

Backhand Block

This is a short, quick, defensive shot usually made from very close to the table. As the ball approaches, line up the body and the racket behind the ball. Contact the ball with an open racket, and move the racket forward with a short thrust, while keeping your eyes on the ball. The follow-through is a short, controlled movement, with a quick return to ready position.

RIGHT HAND   **LEFT HAND**

Strategy

The basic strategy in table tennis is selecting the playing style most natural to you, whether it be smashing, blocking or chopping. There are three basic styles: playing within three feet of the table, within three to six feet of the table, and more than six feet from the table (the defensive players and lobbers). Each style has advantages and disadvantages. I prefer the close-to-the-table style because it allows me to keep control over the table. Whatever style you do select, however, you must believe in it.

Most of the strategy in table tennis today centers around the service, return and first-ball attack. Top players try to win four or five points each time they have the serve, and then break-even on the opponent's serve. Since the coming of the offensive loop drive, the short game has become an important strategic weapon. A ball which drops just over the net and bounces twice on the table is an effective service. Top players try to make the same kind of short return.

During a game, short shots are often used to strategic advantage. The drop shot is used when the opponent has been forced far back from the table. The ball is merely touched with the racket in a way calculated to drop the ball just over the net. Even if it does not win the point, it will help to tire out an opponent and leave him in bad position for the next shot.

The drop shot can also be very effective against lobbers. This is seen mostly in Europe where there are many fine lobbers; however, it is a delicate shot and must be aimed exactly right in order for it to work.

The backhand push is a control shot used to receive serves and gain better position to score the point.

Above all, try to maintain a steady, cool attitude during the game. It is to your opponent's advantage if you lose your temper. If you let him know that you are upset, he will press all the harder and force you to commit foolish errors that will lose you the game.

Drop Shot

From the normal receiving stance, move into position so that the body and racket are right on top of the ball. There is no definite stroke; the drop is primarily a touch shot. With the eyes on the ball, and the racket open, gently move the ball forward to let it drop just over the net. Better players often start with the racket high, as though starting a full stroke, to throw opponents off.

RIGHT HAND   **LEFT HAND**

Drop Shot of a Lob

In preparing for this shot, I have already come around to the side of the table to receive the lob short and to keep the ball short on the return.

It is very important to keep the eyes right on the ball, and line the racket up behind the ball. As the ball bounces and begins to come up high, gently cover the ball with the racket as it comes above the net. With just a slight forward movement of the racket, *feel* the ball over the net. This slight forward movement also constitutes the follow-through.

RIGHT HAND　　**LEFT HAND**

Backhand Push

This shot is made from over the table, with a gentle stroke similar to the chop only shorter. Keep your eyes on the ball and bring the racket up so that it is partially open on contact. Then stroke the racket under the ball to complete the push. The follow-through leaves the arm fully extended.

RIGHT HAND   **LEFT HAND**

OFFICIAL RULES
of the United States
Table Tennis Association

Singles

Table

The table shall be rectangular, 9 ft. (274 cm.) in length, 5 ft. (152.5 cm.) in width; and supported in such a way that its upper surface shall be 2 ft. 6 in. (76 cm.) above the floor, and lie in a horizontal plane. It shall be made of any material yielding a uniform bounce of not less than 8¾ in. (22 cm.) and not more than 9¾ in. (25 cm.) when a standard ball, preferably of medium bounce, is dropped from a height of 12 in. (30.5 cm.) above its surface.

The upper surface of the table, the "playing surface," shall be mat, a very dark color, preferably dark green, with a white line ¾ in. (2 cm.) wide along each edge. The lines at the 5 ft. edges or ends of the playing surface are the "end lines." The lines at the 9 ft. edges or sides of the playing surface are the "side lines." (Note: For center line on table surface see Doubles—TABLE.)

Net and Supports

The playing surface shall be divided into two courts of equal size by a net running parallel to the end lines and 4 ft. 6 in. (137 cm.) from each. The net with its suspension shall be 6 ft. (183 cm.) in length; its upper part along its whole length 6 in. (15.25 cm.) above the playing surface. The lower part of the net, along the whole length, shall be close to the playing surface so that a ball can not pass between them. The net must be suspended by a cord attached at each end to upright posts 6 in. (15.25 cm.) high extending 6 in. (15.25 cm.) outside the side lines, past the table rim.

Ball

The ball shall be round, made of celluloid or a similar plastic, and white but not shiny. It shall not be less than 1.46 in. (37.2 mm.) nor more than 1.50 in. (38.2 mm.) in diameter and shall not weigh less than 37 grains (2.40 gr.) nor more than 39 grains (2.53 gr.)

Racket

The racket may be of any size, shape or weight. Its surface shall be dark-colored and dull. The blade shall be made of continuous wood of even thickness, flat and rigid. If the blade is covered on either side, this covering may be either:

1) plain, ordinary pimpled rubber, with pimples outward, of a total thickness of not more than 2 mm.; or

2) "sandwich," consisting of a layer of cellular rubber surfaced by plain ordinary pimpled rubber—turned outwards or inwards—in which case the total thickness of the covering of either side shall not be more than 4 mm.

When rubber is used on both sides of a racket, the color shall be similar. When wood is used for either side, or for both sides, it should be dark, either naturally or by being stained (not painted) in such a way as not to change the friction-character of its surface.

The part of the blade nearest the handle and gripped by the fingers may be covered with cork or other materials for convenience of grip. In this case, it is to be regarded as part of the handle. If the reverse side of the racket, however, is never used for striking the ball, it may also be covered with cork or any other material convenient for gripping. The limitation of racket cover materials refers *only* to the striking surface. A stroke with a side covered with cork or any other gripping surface would, however, be illegal and result in a loss point.

Play Definition

The player who first strikes the ball during a rally is the *server*.

The player who next strikes the ball during a rally is the *receiver*.

The period during which the ball is in play is called a *rally*.

A rally, the result of which is not scored, is a *let*.

A rally, the result of which is scored, is a *point*.

Good Service

The ball shall be placed on the palm of the free hand, which must be stationary, open and flat, with the fingers together and thumb free. The free hand, while in contact with the ball, shall at all times be above the level of the playing service. Service shall commence by the server tossing the ball, without imparting spin, near vertically upwards so that the ball is visible at all times to the umpire and receiver, and so that it visibly leaves the palm. As the ball is decending from the height of the toss, it shall be struck by the racket in the racket hand of the server so that it touches first the server's court and then, passing directly over or around the net, touches the receiver's court.

If a player, in attempting to serve, misses the ball altogether, it is a lost point because the ball was in play from the moment it left his hand, and a good service has not been made of the ball already in play.

The table surface, or playing area, includes the top edges of the table. A ball in play which strikes these edges is therefore good and still in play. If a ball in play strikes the side of the table-top, below the edge, however, it becomes dead and counts against the last striker. The direction in which the ball travels since it was last struck, its spin, and the direction in which it rebounds from the edge all help to distinguish between a "good" ball that has touched the top edge and a "bad" ball that has made contact below the edge. If the point of contact of the ball occurred at the end or side of the table away from the striker, it must nearly always have been a "good" touch. Only an exceptionally heavy spin could have brought about a contact completely below the edge. If contact occurred on the same side of the table as that from which the ball was struck, it may, however, have occurred below the edge. If the rebound in this case is directly downwards, this is a sign that the contact must have been "bad," i.e. against the side, below the edge.

If the ball, in passing over or around the net, should touch the net or its supports the ball shall, nevertheless, be considered to have passed directly. (Note: "Around the net" shall be considered as the ball passing under or around the projection of the net *and* its supports outside the side lines. The net end should be close enough to the post to prevent the ball from passing between the net and the post. To pass in this way would not constitute "around the net.")

Good Return

A ball having been served or returned in play shall be struck so that it passes directly over or around the net and touches directly the opponent's court. If the ball having been served or returned in play, returns with its own impetus over or around the net, it may be struck, while still in play, so that it touches directly the opponent's court.

In Play

The ball is in play from the moment at which it is tossed in preparation for the serve until:

1) it has touched one court twice consecutively.
2) it has, except in service, touched each court alternately without having been struck by the racket in between.
3) it has been struck by any player more than once consecutively (or, in doubles,

by any player out of proper sequence).

4) it has touched any player or anything that he wears or carries, except his racket hand below the wrist.

5) on the volley it comes in contact with the racket or the racket hand below the wrist.

6) it has touched any object other than the net, supports, or those referred to above.

Let

A rally is a let:

1) if in passing over the net, the ball served touches the net or its supports, provided the service either be otherwise good or volleyed by the receiver. (Note: If the ball in play comes into contact with the racket or racket hand, not yet having touched the playing surface on one side of the net since last being struck on the other side, it shall be said to have been volleyed.)

2) if a service be delivered when the receiver is not ready. The receiver, however, may not be deemed unready if he attempt to strike at the ball.

3) if any player be prevented by an accident, not under his control, from serving a good service or making a good return, or if either player lose the point owing to an accident not within his control.

If the ball splits or becomes otherwise fractured in play, affecting a player's return, the rally is a let. It is the umpire's duty to stop play and to record a let when he has reason to believe that the ball in play is fractured or imperfect. The umpire must also decide those cases in which the faulty ball is clearly fractured in actually going out of play, in no way handicapping the player's return. In these cases, the point should be scored. In doubtful cases, however, the umpire should declare a let.

A moving spectator, a neighboring player, a sudden noise, i.e. any neighboring object in movement (except a partner) should be regarded as an uncontrolled accident, interference from which implies a let. A stationary spectator, fixed seating, the umpire, the light, a nearby table, a continuous sound of even volume, i.e. any relatively constant or motionless hazard, should not be so regarded. Complaints of interference from the latter during play should be regarded as void.

Point

Except as provided above, denoting a let, either player shall lose a point:

1) if the server fails to make a good service.
2) if a good service or a good return having been made by his opponent, he fails to make a good return.
3) if he, or his racket, or anything that he wears or carries moves the playing surface while the ball is in play.
4) if he, or his racket, or anything that he wears or carries move the playing surface while the ball is in play.
5) if his free hand touches the playing surface while the ball is in play.
6) if, before the ball in play shall have passed over the end lines or side lines not yet having touched the playing surface on his side of the table since being struck by his opponent, it comes in contact with him or with anything that he wears or carries.
7) if, at any time, he volleys the ball.

If a game be unfinished fifteen minutes after it has begun, the rest of that game and the remaining games of the match proceed under the Expedite System. Thereafter, if the service and twelve following strokes of the server are returned by good returns of the receiver, the server shall lose the point.

Game

A game shall be won by the player who first wins 21 points, unless both players shall have scored 20 points, when the winner of the game shall be he who first wins two points more than his opponent.

Match

A match shall consist of one game or the best of three or the best of five .games. Play shall be continuous throughout, except that either opposing player is entitled to claim a rest period of not more than five minutes duration between the third and fourth games of a five-game match. (Note: This rule defines a contest between two players or pairs. A contest consisting of a group of individual matches between two sides is usually distinguished as a "team match," and no rest period shall be called.)

Choice of Ends and Service

The choice of ends and the right to be server or receiver in every match shall be decided by toss, provided that, if the winner of the toss choose the right to be server or receiver, the other player shall have the choice of ends, and vice-versa, and provided that the winner of the toss may, if he prefer it, require the other player to make the first choice.

Change of Ends and Service

The player who started at one end in a game shall start at the other in the immediately subsequent game, and so on, until the end of the match. In the last possible game of the match the players shall change ends when first either player reaches the score 10.

After five points, the receiver shall become the server, and the server the receiver, and so on after each five points until the end of the game or the score of 20-all, or if the game be interrupted under the Expedite System (see P O I N T). From the score 20-all, or if the game be interrupted under the Expedite System, the service shall change after each point until the end of the game.

The player who served first in a game shall receive first in the immediately subsequent game, and so on until the end of a match.

Out of Order of Ends or Service

If the players have not changed ends when ends should have been changed, the players shall change ends as soon as the mistake is discovered, unless a game has been completed since the error, whereupon the error shall be ignored. In any circumstances, all points scored before the discovery shall be reckoned.

If a player serve out of his turn, play shall be interrupted as soon as the mistake is discovered and shall continue with that player serving who, according to the sequence established at the beginning of the match, or at the score 10, should be the server at the score that has been reached. In any circumstances, all points scored before the discovery shall be reckoned.

Doubles

The laws for singles shall apply in doubles games, except as outlined here.

Table

The surface of the table shall be divided into two parts by a white line which is ⅛ in. (3 mm.) broad, running parallel with the side lines and distant equally from each of them. This line is termed the center line. (Note: The doubles center line may be permanently marked in full length on the table. This is a convenience and in no way invalidates the table for singles play.)

The part of the table surface on the nearer side of the net and the right of the center line in respect to the server is the server's right half-court, that on the left in respect to him is the server's left half-court. The part of the table surface on the farther side of the net and the left of the center line in respect to the server is the receiver's right half-court, that on the right in respect to the server is the receiver's left half-court.

Good Service

The service shall be delivered as otherwise provided and so that it touches first the server's right half-court or the center line on his side of the net and then, passing directly over or around the net, touches the receiver's right half-court or the center line on his side of the net.

Order of Play

The server shall first make a good service and the receiver a good return. The partner of the server shall then make a good return, then the partner of the receiver shall make a good return. The server shall then make a good return and thereafter each player alternately in that sequence shall make a good return.

Choice of Order of Play

The pair who have the right to serve the first five services in any game shall decide which partner shall do so. In the first game of the match the opposing pair shall then decide similarly which shall be the first receiver. In subsequent games the serving pair shall choose their first server, and the first receiver will then be established automatically to correspond with the first server as provided below.

Order of Service

Throughout each game, except as provided in the second paragraph, the first five services shall be delivered by the selected partner of the pair who have the right to do so and shall be received by the appropriate partner of the opposing pair. The second five services shall be delivered by the receiver of the first five services and received by the partner of the server of the first five services. The third five services shall be delivered by the partner of the server of the first five services and received by the partner of the receiver of the first five services. The fourth five services shall be delivered by the partner of the receiver of the first five services and received by the server of the first five services. And so on, in sequence, until the end of the game or the score 20-all or the introduction of the Expedite System, when the sequence of serving and receiving shall be uninterrupted, but each player shall serve only one service in turn until the end of the game.

In the last possible game of a match, when first either player reaches the score of 10, the receiving pair must alter its order of serving.

In each game of a match the initial order of receiving shall be opposite to that in the preceding game.

Out of Order of Receiving

If a player act as receiver out of turn, play shall be interrupted as soon as the mistake is discovered and shall continue with that player receiving who, according to the sequence established at the beginning of the game or at the score of 10 if that sequence has been changed (see ORDER OF SERVICE), should be receiver at the score which has been reached. In any circumstances, all points scored before the discovery shall be counted.

United States
Table Tennis Association

The United States Table Tennis Association is a non-profit organization functioning through state, district and local associations. The members are people like yourself—people who thoroughly enjoy table tennis. They find more pleasure playing in leagues, clubs and tournaments where style of play, competition and instruction are superior to that found in most basement playrooms.

Membership in the USTTA is available to any person interested in table tennis—champion and beginner alike. The membership fee, with all other USTTA income, is used to support USTTA activities.

For further information about the USTTA —memberships, local associations, copies of the national magazine—or the answer to any table tennis question, write:

United States Table Tennis Association
Box 8587, Kensington Station
Detroit, Michigan 48224

EXERCISES

Warm-up

The following exercises may be used both to warm up for a game or a practice session and to develop table tennis skills.

The Head and Neck Rotation relaxes the head and neck muscles for ease, accuracy and speed in following the ball.

For developing the stroke, the Horizontal Arm Rotation loosens and strengthens the arm for power, reach and follow-through. For more powerful smashes, try the Finger Pull and Palm Press. They strengthen the lower and upper arms respectively. The Wrist and Finger Flex helps in handling the rackets skillfully by loosening the hand, wrist and lower arm.

For strengthening the legs and developing speed in movement and positioning, the following three exercises are excellent: the Knee Thrust loosens the whole leg, for agility; the Side Step develops footwork; and the Side Jump develops the balance and coordination needed to move the body quickly into position as a single unit for a return of the ball.

For both footwork and paddle skill, and as a good all-around warm-up, try the Ankle Twist and the Wrist Shake.

Head and Neck Rotation

Plant your feet firmly, place your hands on your hips and stretch your head around as far as possible and back again. For greatest benefit, turn your head slowly and purposefully, trying to reach the furthest points of this imaginary circle.

This exercise will make it easier for you to follow the ball and keep your head and eyes close to the stroke.

Horizontal Arm Rotation

Using the body as an axis, swing your arms slowly from side to side reaching out and gradually stretching to form big circles. Let your legs and torso follow your arm movements, but try to keep your head and feet stationary. This movement is similar to a very full baseball swing with an equally full follow-through.

Finger Pull

With the fingers together and bent toward the palms, interlock finger-tips. Attempt to pull hands apart, forcing the fingers against each other. Try to keep the pressure up for from thirty to sixty seconds each time, for best results. Follow this exercise with the Palm Press.

The Finger Pull is designed to strengthen the lower arm muscles. It is used by the Orientals to develop more powerful smashes.

Palm Press

The principle of this exercise is much the same as with the Finger Pull, except that it is performed by pressing rather than by pulling. Simply place the heels of your hands together, heading in opposite directions, and push them against each other as hard as possible for thirty to sixty seconds.

This exercise strengthens the upper arm and, like the Finger Pull, is good for the strong attacker.

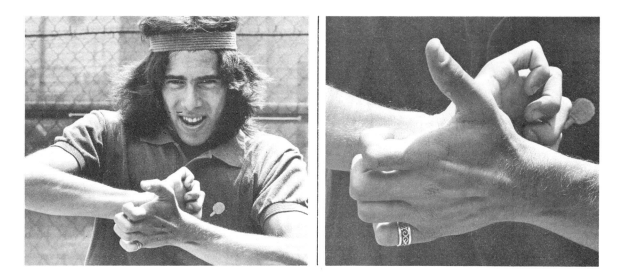

Wrist and Finger Flex

Clasp the hands together. Move one hand forward from the wrist, forcing the other hand down and back at the wrist, then reverse. Alternate hands as fast as possible, but keep the rest of the arm steady as the wrist flexes back and forth.

This is a very good loosening warm-up to use before a match.

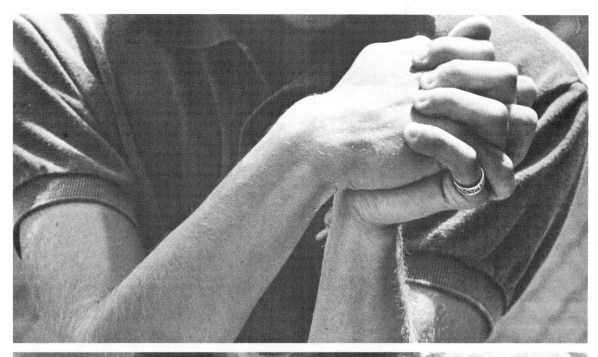

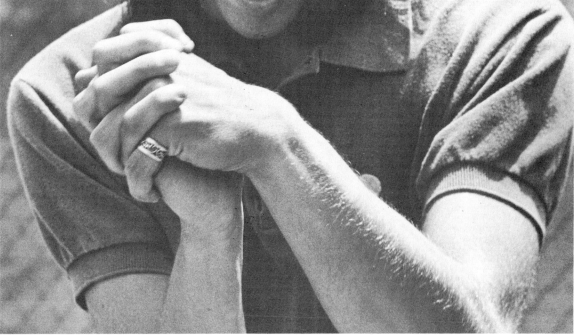

Knee Thrust

The Knee Thrust is a combination leg exercise. First place your hands on your knees and push in. This loosens the knee and upper leg muscles. Next, go into a squatting position and bounce twice, to loosen the calf and lower leg muscles.

This is also a good pre-match warm-up.

Side Step

Start in a low crouch, as if ready to play, legs well apart and arms extended in front for balance. Quickly slide the left leg in toward the right, transfer your weight, and move the right leg out to the side, returning again to the crouch position. Next, reverse the procedure, bringing the right leg in toward the left. Continue the exercise, moving quickly from side to side, and staying as low as possible, for two counts of ten.

This exercise is also practice for the quick side-to-side motion needed in a game. The movement of the feet should be slide-like, one at a time, and very fast, to enable a player to get quickly and smoothly from one side of the table to the other. Oriental players, whose penhold grip limits them to forehand strokes, rely on this smooth, swift movement to enable them to cover the entire table.

Side Jump

Start with both hands back, feet together and legs crouched. Jump as far as possible to one side, keeping the feet together and staying low. You will find your hands coming forward during the jump for balance. Jump back and forth for two counts of ten.

This exercise develops agility and strength in the legs, balance during motion, and helps to coordinate the movements of the upper body and the legs so that the entire body moves as a unit. It is also a particularly good warm-up exercise.

Ankle Twist

Spread your legs comfortably apart. Standing on the balls of your feet, move the heel of one foot inward and outward rapidly, as if you were mashing out a cigarette butt. First twist each foot alternately, then do them both together. Try to do the Ankle Twist for thirty to sixty seconds. It is a fine pre-match warm-up exercise, loosening the ankles and readying the legs to move.

Wrist Shake

This simple exercise is best done in conjunction with the Ankle Twist. Let your arms hang loosely at your sides and shake your wrists. Continue until your wrists are thoroughly loose. What the fingers do is up to you.

Conditioning

You may be quite surprised to find yourself becoming winded, aching and fatigued after only a few dozen rallies. Table tennis has developed over the years into a strenuous game, demanding quickness, energy and endurance from today's serious players. The following exercises are designed to help you get into shape to play your best. If you are really out of condition, however, ease into the exercises. Start off by doing them only once or twice during each exercise session, or to a count of five or ten, rather than the full recommended amount; and work your way up.

Two of the exercises, the Around the House and the Toe Touch to the Side, condition the body to take the strain of long, hard play. The Half Sit-Up, the Back Stretch and the High Jump loosen and stretch shoulder and upper back muscles, as well as strengthen leg and thigh muscles, to allow a player to take and maintain the low crouch playing stance for an extended period of time.

Around the House

Place your hands on your hips and spread your legs well apart. Bend forward at the waist, lowering your head as far as possible. Then, moving slowly and deliberately, trace an imaginary circle with your upper body. Reach with the head to make the circle as large as possible, but keep the legs in the same position. Swing slowly all the way around counterclockwise, then reverse direction and return clockwise to the front position. Around and back is one complete movement; do it ten times.

This exercise is designed to condition the upper body to withstand long periods of hard play. It also strengthens the back and thigh muscles and in general loosens and relaxes the whole upper body.

Around the House (continued)

Toe Touch to Side

Stand erect with your feet spread well apart. Bend at the waist to the right. Touch your right foot with your right hand. Straighten up, then bend to the left and touch your left foot with your left hand. Repeat, alternating sides for two counts of twenty.

This exercise stretches the muscles along both sides of the torso, and also the upper thigh muscles. It develops stamina and tones the muscles used in reaching for balls hit to one side or the other during a game.

Half Sit-Up with Partner

Sit upright, with your legs stretched out in front of you and flat against the floor. The partner stands in back and places his hands heavily on your shoulders. As you extend your arms toward your toes and attempt to touch the bridges of your feet, your partner should add the final touch by pushing down on your shoulders. Two counts of ten is plenty for this exercise.

This exercise is excellent for enabling a player to stay in a low crouch for an entire game. It also develops stamina in the legs and stretches and loosens the leg muscles as well as the muscles in the shoulder and back.

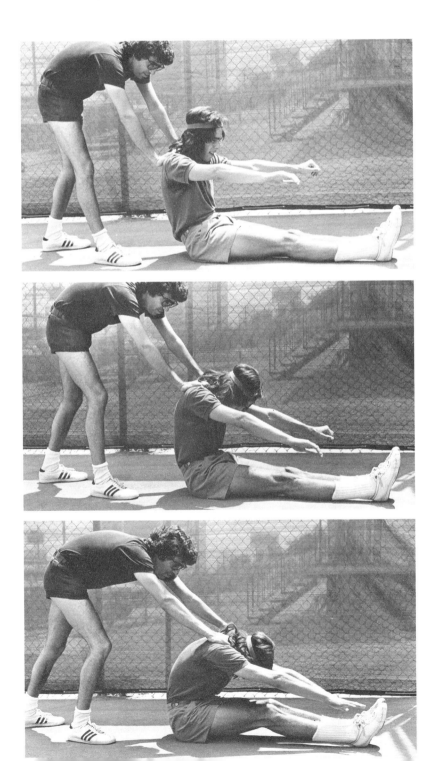

Back Stretch with Partner

Stand back to back with your partner and interlock hands as shown. Lean forward and gradually lift your partner's weight onto your shoulders. Be sure to move very slowly so as not to flip your partner onto the ground. Once your partner is securely positioned on your back, shake him up and down for a count of ten. Then it is your partner's turn to raise you on his back.

This exercise releases back tension for the partner being raised, making the back muscles loose and flexible. The partner on the bottom benefits also by having the back, shoulder and thigh muscles strengthened.

High Jump

Start crouched very low. Then, quickly, leap as high as possible, bringing both legs up together. Spread your arms for balance. Repeat this procedure for two counts of ten. You'll feel this one right away!

The High Jump quickly develops stamina in the leg and stomach muscles.

About GLENN COWAN

Table tennis champ Glenn Cowan was born in New York City on August 25, 1951. By the age of eleven, he was actively involved in a variety of sports—winning a gold medal for swimming, playing on the junior high tennis and baseball teams, and bowling. Glenn's budding interest in the sport of table tennis was encouraged by his father, and they enjoyed many lively matches at the family home in New Rochelle, New York. One year later, twelve-year-old Glenn Cowan won the Westchester County Table Tennis Tournament.

The Cowan family moved to Los Angeles in 1965, where Glenn attended University High School, and continued to play table tennis. At the United States Championships in San Diego in 1967, Glenn won the National Junior Group. Two years later, at the age of seventeen, he attended his first international competition, the World's Championship Table Tennis Matches in Munich, Germany.

Glenn Cowan represented California at the U.S. National Championships in Detroit in November 1970. Defeating five of the top-ranked U.S. players, he was chosen to accompany the U.S. Table Tennis Team to Nagoya in March 1971 to compete in the World Championship. Then came the surprise invitation by the Red Chinese government, the U.S. Table Tennis Team visit to mainland China, and the hopeful start of "Ping Pong diplomacy."

Glenn Cowan is presently studying at Santa Monica College, and taking film courses at the Southern California Film Institute.